the art of group talk

HOW TO LEAD BETTER CONVERSATIONS WITH KIDS

"That shirt makes you look big."
LEROY, KINDERGARTEN

———

"Do you live at church?"
JUAN, 2ND GRADE

———

**"I've never lied before . . .
but my sister has."**
WALKER, 1ST GRADE

———

**"How come Kyle's Elf on the Shelf brings him
gifts and mine doesn't?"**
PRESTON, KINDERGARTEN

———

"Last week, my uncle killed a snake and put it in his freezer."
AVA, 4TH GRADE

"One time I didn't study for a test so I prayed to God to help me and I got a B+."
ELLIE, 5TH GRADE

"Jesus came to give us hope! I hope that I go to the Bahamas."
JAMAL, 1ST GRADE

The Art of Group Talk: Kids
Published by Orange, a division of The reThink Group, Inc.
5870 Charlotte Lane, Suite 300
Cumming, GA 30040 U.S.A.

The Orange logo is a registered trademark of The reThink Group, Inc.

All Scripture quotations, unless otherwise noted, are taken from the *Holy Bible, New International Version®. NIV®.* Copyright © 1973, 1978, 1984 by International Bible Society. Used by permission of Zondervan.

Other Orange products are available online and direct from the publisher. Visit our website at www.WhatIsOrange.org for more resources like these.

ISBN: 978-1-63570-902-5

©2017 The reThink Group, Inc.

Writers: Afton Phillips, Adam Duckworth
Contributing Writers: Elle Campbell
Lead Small Editing Team: Mike Jefferies, Steph Whitacre, Elloa Davis, Adriana Howard
Art Direction: Ryan Boon
Project Manager: Nate Brandt
Design: FiveStone

Printed in the United States of America
First Edition 2017

1 2 3 4 5 6 7 8 9 10

04/20/17

Table
of
Contents

Foreword

This is a book about how to have better conversations with kids.

Because, as a small group leader, you lead a conversation with kids every single week. Conversations about . . .
their lives.
their dreams.
their friends.
their imaginary friends.
and their definitely-not friends.

And sometimes, you even manage to lead conversations about faith.

This is a book to remind you that your small group conversations—even the ones that don't go exactly as planned—**really matter.**

But there are a few ways to make your conversations **matter even more.**

create a
safe place

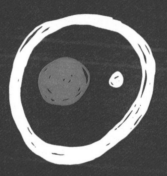

clarify their
faith as
they grow

Introduction

You probably signed up to be a small group leader (or SGL for short) because you wanted . . .
to make a big difference.
to change the world.
to invest in a few kids so you could help them develop a lifelong, authentic kind of faith.

We call that **leading small.**

Maybe you didn't know exactly what you were getting into when you signed up to be an SGL, but you probably at least knew this:

Leading a *small group* means leading a weekly small group *conversation.*

Kind of obvious, right?

But the truth is, figuring out how to lead a conversation with a group of kids isn't always obvious. It's definitely not like leading a conversation with a group of adults.

I learned this the hard way. When I (Afton) signed up to be an SGL, I had some pretty big expectations for how those weekly small group conversations should look. At the time, I thought leading a small group of kids would be pretty much like leading a conversation with a bunch of me's—but smaller. And louder. And more giggly.

Before I became an SGL, I expected to lead small group conversations where every kid . . .
paid attention.
participated.
maybe even cried
(but not because they poked themselves in the eye with a crayon).

^ attempted to lead
But then I led my first small group of kids and, well, you can guess how that went.

If you've been an SGL for more than five minutes, you already know what I learned that day—that leading a conversation with a group of kids doesn't always live up to your expectations. (Especially if your expectations looked anything like mine.)

In fact, if you have any SGL experience whatsoever, it's probably safe to say that **you know what it's like to have a small group conversation totally bomb.**

Maybe you led a small group where your kids weren't exactly talkative.
You tried to get the conversation moving, but you were met with . . .
the sound of crickets.
blank stares.
the tops of their heads as they try to break a record for how many crayons they can get through in a single group hour.

Or maybe they were a little *too* talkative.
Maybe you were forced to scream the discussion questions at the top of your lungs while they . . .
wrestled each other on the floor.
hid behind the tech booth.
asked you to judge their cartwheel competition.

Or maybe they were just the right amount of talkative, but

you're convinced your volunteer training didn't prepare you for the kinds of topics they wanted to talk about.

When leading a small group of kids, sometimes you have to beg them to say something—*anything*.

But more often than not, you wish they would lose the ability to speak altogether.

And maybe sometimes, you probably head home after a particularly challenging small group and wonder,
"Did I say the right thing?
Were they even listening?
Do these conversations matter at all?"

If you've ever been there, you're not alone. Everyone who has ever led a small group of kids has, at some point, wondered if they were completely wasting their time. (We don't exactly have the data to support this claim, but we're still pretty sure it's true.)

Especially on days when your group spends more time turning their activity pages into paper airplanes than engaging in a conversation about faith, those questions are understandable.

But the next time a conversation goes completely off the rails and you're wondering if you're a terrible small group leader—or if you think leading a small group of elementary schoolers should be classified as a new form of torture— there are two things we hope you'll remember.

Here's the first:

Your small group conversations matter.

And we don't just mean those once-in-a-lifetime conversations where everyone decides to accept Jesus into their hearts simultaneously—we mean every small group conversation.

The one when Walker hid behind the furniture? It mattered.
The one where you didn't finish any activities? It mattered.
The one where your group wanted to know if God could
make a mozzarella stick so hot even He couldn't eat it? It
mattered.
And the conversation you're about to lead this week? Yep.
It's going to matter, too.

The good news for SGLs like you and me is that the quality
of the conversation you'll lead this week won't determine
your ultimate success or failure as a small group leader.
Sometimes a conversation will bomb, and that's okay,
because that one conversation isn't the only conversation
you'll ever have with your few.

In the book *Lead Small*, we talked about the importance
of showing up predictably—weekly, in fact—for your few.
Actually, it's the very first thing we talked about. That's
because showing up predictably, consistently, and regularly
in the lives of the kids you lead is the foundation of leading
your small group (and of leading a small group conversation).

When you show up predictably, you begin to understand
that one conversation doesn't determine your success as a
small group leader. Instead, you realize that your success
is actually determined by every small group conversation
you've ever had, added up and then multiplied by factors
we haven't yet identified. Because when you combine the
dozens, or hundreds, of conversations you've had with
your small group, they equal something pretty significant.
They equal . . .

Relationships.
Trust.
Influence.

So, you see, your small group conversations matter—even those conversations that are difficult or frustrating, or that don't *exactly* go according to plan. They matter because each of those weekly small group conversations are part of something bigger.

Ten years from now, the kids in your small group will probably not remember much of what was said during your small group conversations. But they will remember how those consistent, weekly conversations resulted in a relationship that made an impact on their lives. That's the power of showing up consistently.

So next time a small group conversation doesn't quite meet your expectations, remember: **your small group conversations matter—maybe more than you think.**

But here's the second thing we hope you remember:

Your small group conversations can matter more.

In fact, that's what this book is all about—practical ideas and strategies to help you make the most out of your conversations with your small group.

While the one conversation you lead this week will not determine your success as a small group leader, it will affect it. The influence you're building through your weekly conversations is important, but if you never actually use that influence to help your few build a more authentic faith . . . then you've missed it.

But you're not going to miss it. We know that because you're reading a book about how to make your small group conversations matter more, and that's a pretty good sign. You're already on your way to leading better conversations—conversations where the kids in your group will not only be able to engage, but will be able to . . .

be themselves.
share their doubts.
ask tough questions.
share their struggles.

It isn't always easy to lead those kinds of conversations, though. So if you've ever looked at your small group of kids and wished you knew . . .
what to say
what not to say
what to ask
how to ask it
when to speak
when to listen
how to make them talk
how to make them stop talking
. . . then keep reading.

We don't know everything about leading conversations for kids, but we've spent a lot of time leading small groups, talking to other small group leaders, and learning how to lead small groups better. And now we want to take the things we've learned and share them with you. Things that, we hope, will help you make the most of your limited opportunities to lead a conversation with your small group.

So remember.

Your small group conversations matter. They matter because, with every conversation you lead, you're building a relationship with your few that has the potential to influence them for a lifetime.

But your small group conversations can matter more.
And here's how . . .

1

chapter
one
prepare

Prepare

Picture this.

It's Saturday night. You've had a get-it-done weekend filled with cleaning your car, going to soccer games, shopping for groceries, mowing the lawn, and walking the dog, and your head finally hits the pillow for a restful night's sleep. Then your eyes spring open.

You realize . . .

You have to set your alarm for an unreasonably early hour to lead a small group of kids in the morning.

Ever been there? We sure have. Now, don't get us wrong. We love our small groups. We care about them. We're committed to them. We want to have great conversations together. But . . . well, we're not always as prepared for our conversations as we should be.

Maybe you can relate. Maybe you know what it's like to fly through the church doors, desperately searching through your phone for the email from your children's pastor about what in the world you're supposed to do and talk about in small group this week. You skim through as much as you can before kids show up, but then here comes your early bird. And it's a little tough to concentrate when your early bird is talking so much. And then another shows up. And another. And before you know it, they're all talking to you a million miles a minute and you're grunting out *uh-huh's* as you take in as much information from the curriculum as you can, wondering the whole time why your children's pastor handed you a baggie of loose glitter when you walked in and secretly hoping you run out of time before that activity.

You make it through your small group time, but maybe the best part of the group was the very end, when you didn't have a sheet of paper in your face and you just talked to your few about what they heard in the story. Sure, it got the job done. If you've been with your group for some time, maybe your kids don't even notice how much you were winging it. But on your way home, you might have wondered, *What kind of conversation could we have had if I'd been just a little more prepared?*

If we're honest, we've all had weeks like that. It happens. But if you want to get serious about making your conversations with your few matter more (and we know you do), then we've got to talk about **preparation** because the first step in leading a better small group conversation is to . . .

PREPARE

We know. We know!

You're a volunteer. You don't get paid to lead a small group. You've inserted yourself into the busy and rapidly expanding worlds of a few kids and you're going to get absolutely nothing in return, except maybe a free T-shirt and some sugary donuts. You're already giving a ton of your time by showing up and leading these conversations, but now we're suggesting you should spend time *preparing* for those conversations, too?

Well, yes.
But it's simple. We promise!

There are four things you can do to prepare for your small group conversations each week. And you can do them all from your couch.

If you want to prepare for your small group conversation,
READ your email.

We know email is outdated. That's what our kids tell us anyway. But we're not kids. We're grown ups. And since we're grown ups, we should probably still be checking—and reading—our emails.

We don't mean those emails about buy-one-get-one jeans or 25-percent-off sale items. Those emails probably won't help you prepare for your small group (although they might make your wardrobe a little bit cooler).

We're talking about emails from your children's pastor.

We may not know your children's pastor, but we're going to assume a few things about what they do every week. We're guessing your children's pastor or coach . . .
cares about your small group conversation.
thinks about your small group conversation.
has a plan for your small group conversation.
emails you the plan for your small group conversation.

Hopefully, that email from your children's pastor tells you important information like what they'll be teaching and what you'll be asking when you get to small group each week.

Ring any bells?
No?
Then you probably need to update your contact information in the church database or check your Recently Deleted folder.

But if you've checked, and double checked, and are absolutely positive your children's pastor doesn't send you a weekly email, try not to be too hard on them. We're sure they really want you to succeed as a small group leader! So don't get mad. If your children's pastor doesn't send you a weekly email, try this . . .

1.   Open your email app.
2.   Write a new message to your children's pastor.
3.   Say something like this:

> Hey _____! You know what would be really awesome? I would love to get an email every week, maybe a few days in advance, that helps me get ready for my small group. I think my small group conversations could be a lot better if I had a little time to **think about what we're teaching** and **read my small group activities and questions** before I get to small group. What do you think?

Pretty simple, right?

And if your children's pastor already sends you a weekly email, your job is even easier:

1.   Open their email.
2.   Read it.

If you already do this, way to go! You are a very prepared SGL. And hey, here's a thought. If you love getting those emails in advance, take a second to hit "Reply" to your childrens pastor's weekly email and say, "Thanks!" They'll love to hear their weekly emails aren't disappearing into inbox oblivion.

If you want this week's small group conversation to matter more, you need to know what the small group conversation will be about—you know, *before* you walk in the door. **Prepare for your small group conversation. READ YOUR EMAIL.**

**If you want to prepare for your small group conversation,
REHEARSE what you'll say.**

Have you ever had an **imaginary conversation**?

Sure you have. Maybe it was when you were . . .
getting ready for a first date.
preparing for a job interview.
thinking of some killer comebacks for that troll on
Facebook.

Having imaginary conversations simply means mentally
rehearsing what you're going to say before you say it.
Imaginary conversations are helpful when you're preparing
for a date and they're helpful when you're preparing for
your not-so-imaginary small group conversations, too.

We're not saying you should memorize lines or write a
monologue for your small group conversation. In fact,
please don't. We're just saying that **what you say can
probably be said better if you rehearse what you're
going to say (or not say) before you say it.**

Just like . . .
a surgeon practices before a procedure
a lawyer practices for a trial
a pilot practices in a flight simulator
you should practice for your small group conversation.

As an SGL, having an imaginary conversation means trying
to anticipate how your small group conversation will go
before small group so you'll be less likely to be caught off-
guard *during* small group.

So how do you do that? Well, once you've read your email
from your children's pastor, ask yourself a few questions
about what they'll be teaching, like . . .

- What do my kids know, think, or feel about this topic?
- How does this topic relate to specific situations in their lives right now?
- Could this topic raise any challenging questions or strong opinions?

Next, take a look at your small group questions for the week and ask yourself a few questions **about what you'll be discussing**, like . . .

- Will these small group questions make sense to them?
- How are my kids going to answer these questions?
- Will they feel comfortable answering them honestly?
- Do I need to rephrase any of these questions for my group?
- Are there any activities I should change that would work better for my group?
- Is there at least one activity to get my movers moving?!

See? It's simple, but it's so important! When you have a weekly imaginary conversation with yourself, you'll be able to better . . .
clarify your thoughts.
refine your words.
anticipate their responses.
lead the conversation.

Remember, if you want this week's small group conversation to matter more, you want to think about how the conversation will go *before* the conversation begins. **Prepare for your small group conversation.**

REHEARSE WHAT YOU'LL SAY.

**If you want to prepare for your small group conversation,
PACK a survival kit.**

No, we don't mean bandages and disinfectant (although, with kids, that's actually not a bad idea).

We mean the kind of supplies that will help you rescue your small group conversation in the event of emergencies like . . .
out of control extroverts.
awkward silences.
irrelevant rabbit trails.
general chaos.

 We'll talk about how to use these supplies later in this book. **Just look for this symbol.** For now, just trust us. You'll need:

- A confetti popper
- A stack of icebreaker questions
- A noise maker
- A stress ball
- A zipper lock bag
- A deck of cards
- Candy
- Pens
- Paper

Remember, if you want this week's small group conversation to matter more, you want to be ready for anything. **Prepare for your small group conversation. PACK A SURVIVAL KIT.**

If you want to prepare for your small group conversation,
PRAY for your few.

If you're anything like us, praying for your small group is, unfortunately, sometimes more of an afterthought than a vital part of your weekly preparation. Some weeks, you may only manage a hurried, well-intentioned plea to God on the way to small group. Other weeks, the only time you might pray for your few is *during* your small group.

But no matter how many times you've prayed for your few in the last week, month, or year, we've discovered there are at least two reasons why praying for your small group should be an every-week kind of thing.

Pray for your few because they need it. Do you remember what it was like for you to be a kid? It's hard. Like, really hard. Besides school, sports, siblings, competitions, parents, gossip, and everything else your few are dealing with, every kid is also wrestling with big questions about who they are, why they matter, what they believe, and who they'll become. But we want to create a safe place where those big questions are encouraged. We want every kid to grow up in a healthy environment so they can discover who they are. So as you prepare for your small group conversation each week, don't forget to pray for your few. They need it.

But there's another reason you should pray for your few.

Pray for your few because you need it. When you pray for someone else, it's usually because you want God to do something for them. But what if, when God told us to pray for each other (which He did quite often), He had a second purpose in mind? What if He designed prayer in such a way that praying for someone else didn't just result in change for *them*? What if it changes *us*, too?

When we pray for someone else, we learn to . . .
consider their needs.
imagine their world.
feel their emotions.
understand their perspective.

In other words, **when you pray for the kids you lead,
you develop more compassion for them.** And as an SGL,
you'll need that compassion when . . .
the conversation bombs.
the activity is a fail.
they ask a tough question.
they hurt someone's feelings.

As you prepare for your small group this week, don't let
prayer be an afterthought. Make it a habit. Remember, if
you want this week's small group conversation to matter
more, you want to have a conversation with God *before*
you have a conversation with your few. **Prepare for your
small group conversation. PRAY FOR YOUR FEW.**

So there you have it. Four ways to prepare for your small
group conversation every week. We said it would be
simple, right?
Read your email.
Rehearse what you'll say.
Pack an emergency kit.
Pray for your few.

And now that you're (mostly) prepared for your small group
conversation, let's talk about how to lead that conversation.

QUIZ:

HOW WELL DO YOU PREPARE FOR YOUR SMALL GROUP?

Throughout this book you'll find a few quizzes that we've created as self-evaluation tools. Write in your answers (or just think them), and at the end of this book, you'll be able to see which areas of group conversation you're stellar at as well as the areas you might have a little room to grow in.

Answer honestly and have fun!

Did you get an email from your children's pastor this week? Did you read it?

QUIZ

Do you pray for your few regularly? You know, other than the times they're crying in front of you about not being able to whistle?

Do you usually know what your conversation is going to be about before you arrive?

QUIZ

Speaking of arriving, do you usually show up on time—
or, better yet, a little bit early? (In other words, do you
get there in time for donuts with chocolate sprinkles or
have to settle with plain?)

Do you know the topic so well that you could lead your
small group conversation with your eyes closed? (Well,
we're not saying you should. Because that would be
weird. Keep your eyes open. But could you lead your
group without looking at your small group questions?)

2

chapter
two
connect

Connect

(Talk about something FUN)

Now that you've . . .
read your email
rehearsed what you'll say
packed your emergency kit
prayed for your few
. . . you're ready! It's time to finally lead a small group
conversation.

But wait.

What about the kids in your group?
Are they ready for your conversation?

Right now, the kids you lead are probably not thinking
about your next small group conversation. More than likely,
they're thinking about . . .
that slumber party they got invited to.
what color their soccer trophy might be.
how many days there are until Christmas.
when they can have more screen time.

We don't mean to discourage you. It's not that your few
don't care about you, your small group, or their faith. It's
just that they have a lot of other things on their minds.

And that's okay! You don't need your few to come to small
group ready to talk only about forgiveness, prayer, or the
book of Ephesians. You need them to come to small group
ready to talk about *anything*—especially the stuff that

matters to them. Even if what matters to them is what color their soccer trophy might be.

In the first few minutes of your small group conversation, your few don't need your few to immediately dive into that week's discussion questions. **They just need to connect.**

Don't forget that leading a small group is about something much bigger than discussion questions. It's about the relationships you're building over time. But you'll never build a great small group relationship—or have a great small group conversation—if you can't connect first.

How you connect with your small group is simple. For an SGL like you, it may even be obvious. But just so we're all on the same page, let's put it this way:

Before you talk about faith with your small group, you should spend a little time talking about their week.

Before you ask them to be vulnerable, you should probably ask what they're doing this weekend.

And before you tell them to participate, you should make sure they know you're happy to see them.

Here's the point: **Before a kid can ENGAGE in a conversation about a God who cares about them, they may need to CONNECT with people who care about them.**

2.1

If you want your small group conversations to matter more,

connect with them

Connect
with them

If you're leading a small group of kids, you're probably not a kid. You may have been one at some point, but I'm guessing you're not anymore. And since you're not a kid, it's probably not always going to be easy to connect with the kids in your group.

That's because they're not like you. Whether it's the music you listen to, the things you worry about, or the number of emojis you text each day, you and your few are very different people. At least, I hope so. Because they're kids. And you're not.

And they're not like you used to be. You may remember what it was like to be a kid, but things aren't like they were when you were their age. Even though Furbys, Mario Kart, and Lunchables are still around, they're different than they used to be. Whether you're in your eighties or your twenties, the world has changed quite a bit since you were a kid.

So while it may not always be easy to connect with the kids in your small group, if you want your small group conversations to matter more, you've got to start by making a weekly connection with each of your few. If you want your small group to open up, they need to feel connected to you.

Here are three ways to get started . . .

1. CONNECT BEFORE SMALL GROUP

If conversation comes easily for your small group, you probably know what it's like to look at the clock and realize small group ends in five minutes and your group is still answering the question, "What's the best thing you did this week?"

And if chitchat isn't exactly your small group's favorite hobby, you've probably had weeks when success looked like getting your group to speak in full sentences.

If either of these situations sound familiar to you, whether you wish your small group time was twice as long or half as short, you might have a connection problem. But don't worry. It has an easy solution.
Connect with your few before small group.

Some kids have a lot to say to you—more things than could possibly be covered during your small group time. When you connect with those kids before small group, you give them time to share their stories before your small group conversation begins.

Other kids need some time to warm up before they open up to you. When you connect with those kids before small group, you give them time to get comfortable so they're ready to share when your small group conversation begins.

If you want to make the most of your small group conversation, it's probably a good idea to connect with your few before your small group conversation begins. You might want to try . . .
meeting them at the door.
singing alongside them during worship.
checking in with parents during the week.
sitting with them during the teaching.

Making small connections early can make a big impact on your conversation later. Don't let the first time you connect with your small group be the moment your small group conversation starts. **Connect with them before small group begins.**

2. CONNECT WITH NEW KIDS

Have you ever been to a party where you knew no one? Sure, we all have at some point. Imagine that awkward scenario that you went through is the same thing a new kid goes through every time you have a new kid in small group. When you think about it like that, you put yourself in their shoes.

At some point, chances are someone new will join your small group. And that's a great thing! But let's be honest. It can also be a challenge to add someone new to your group. Will they feel welcome? Will your few like them? Will they have anything in common?

If these are the questions running through your mind, imagine the questions running through your new kids. When you're a kid, being the new kid can be pretty scary. That's why it's up to you to make them feel . . .
welcome.
safe.
liked.
celebrated.

SMALL GROUP SURVIVAL KIT: CONFETTI POPPER
Remember that emergency kit we told you to pack? Here's the first thing on your list. A confetti popper. When someone new joins your group, it's your job to help them feel connected. Celebrate their first week in your group with a confetti popper!

In other words, connect with new kids. Here are a few tips you might want to try . . .

Remember their name. If this doesn't seem like a big deal, it's because you've never seen the look on a kid's face when they realize you've forgotten their name. And you can only say "buddy" and "sweetheart" so many times before they catch on. Next time a new kid shows up for small group, here's a tip:

1. Say their name out loud.
2. Repeat it.
3. And repeat it again.

Like this: "Your name's Ella? It's so great to meet you. Where do you go to school, Ella?" Repeating her name will help you remember it. And it will let her know you remember it, too.

Learn about them. Most kids will be hesitant to join your small group for the first time. So to help them feel comfortable, learn more about them. Ask about their hobbies, school, family, and interests. No matter what's going on around you, make them feel like the most important person in the room.

Find common ground. As you learn about who they are, look for ways to connect their experiences with yours. If they love animals, tell them about your pet hedgehog. If they play tennis, tell them about your terrible hand-eye coordination.
And if they love Shopkins but you aren't exactly sure what that is, Google it.

When a new kid joins your small group, remember, it's your job to help them feel connected. Their experience at church is impacted by their experience with you. So don't just connect with the kids you see every week. **Connect with new kids too.**

3. CONNECT DURING SMALL GROUP

No matter how hard you try to connect with each of the kids in your small group *before* small group begins, there will be weeks when you can't . . .
hug every kid.
hear every story.
catch up on every detail.

So as your small group time begins, use those first few moments to make a quick connection with the kids you haven't connected with yet.

You might be tempted to dive right into your small group conversation and activities. We get it. You've got a lot to accomplish and you probably have that one kid who's always late but *really really really* wants to tell you about his dog before group starts. But when you take the time to connect with every kid, you're not wasting precious small group time. You're laying a foundation that the rest of your conversation will be built on.

So when small group begins, don't rush your few into the activities. **Connect with them during small group.**

Because if you want this week's small group conversation to matter more, your few need to feel connected to you. **CONNECT WITH THEM.**

2.2

If you want your small group conversations to matter more, help them

connect with each other

Connect with each other

As a small group leader, you're a big deal. You give your few a place to belong. You show them what God is like. You love them, lead them, teach them, and coach them. Without SGLs like you, small groups wouldn't work. Your few need you!

But they also need **each other.**

If you look back at the earliest churches, what you'll see is pretty interesting. You'll see no buildings. No choir rooms. No praise bands. There were no children's programs. No Sunday school classes.

There was simply community. Genuine, pure, tight-knit, nothing-to-hide, kill-my-best-goat-for-you kind of community.

The church wasn't a place. The church was a group.

As an SGL, it's your job to cultivate that kind of community.

To give your few
a tribe
a safe place
a small group.

But if you're going to create that kind of community, it's

not enough for your few to connect with you. They need to connect with each other, too.

Oh, but—they're kids. So they may need a little help from you.

They need you to connect them with each other.

1. CONNECT THEM WITH AN ICEBREAKER

You may have spent some time before small group connecting with each of the kids. But now that small group has started, this may be the first time this week they've all connected with one another.

So to help them connect
and get the conversation started,
ask an icebreaker question.

Maybe you ask a silly question like . . .

- Would you rather eat a cottage cheese taco or a yogurt hot dog?
- Unicorns. Real or fake? Explain your view.
- If you got to name the next dinosaur, what would you name it?

Or maybe it's a question about their week, like . . .

- What were your HIGHS and LOWS from last week?
- What made you MAD, SAD, and GLAD this week?
- What's happened since we saw you last?

Or maybe it's a get-to-know-you question, like . . .

- What's one thing no one here knows about you?
- If you could travel anywhere in the world, where would you go?
- If I gave you $1,000, what would you spend it on first?

SMALL GROUP SURVIVAL KIT: ICEBREAKER QUESTIONS

Here's the next thing on your packing list. It's not easy to come up with icebreaker questions on the spot. Trust us. We know. We've tried. They're much easier to come up with when you're not being stared at by a group of antsy third graders (and when you have access to Google). Write down a few of your favorite icebreaker questions and stash them in your Emergency Kit for later.

A good icebreaker question will give your few a chance to . . .
talk about themselves (that means no "yes or no" questions).
learn something new about each other (which happens pretty easily when they're talking about themselves).
laugh together (so maybe ask something other than "what's your favorite Bible verse?").

Because if they don't laugh together, they'll probably never feel comfortable enough to talk with each other about their questions, their doubts, or their life experiences.
So help your few connect with each other. **Connect them with an icebreaker.**

2. CONNECT THEM THROUGH THEIR INTERESTS

Maybe your small group has a lot in common. Maybe they . . .
have all the same hobbies.
laugh at all the same jokes.
like all the same flavors of goldfish.

But probably not.

Most likely, you're probably leading a small group of kids who are all very different. In that case, it's your job as their SGL to help them discover what they have in common.

Maybe they all love puppies . . . or Star Wars. . . or Frappuccinos . . . or Pokemon. If you already know something they all have in common, point out that connection.

If you're not sure what they have in common, turn it into a game. Put five minutes on the clock and challenge them to find one thing they all have in common.

And if you're pretty sure they have absolutely nothing in common, try watching a video of cats. Cat videos bring everyone together.

So help your few connect with each other. **Connect them through their interests.** (And cat videos.)

3. CONNECT THEM WITH SOMEONE NEW

It's not always easy for kids to connect with someone new. Even inside your small group, you've probably noticed that some kids don't connect quite as well as others. And that's okay. You can't force your kids to be friends, but you can encourage them to make a new connection.

You might want to try . . .
splitting into pairs to answer an icebreaker question.
splitting into *new* pairs for the next question.
splitting into *new* new pairs after that.
splitting into even more new pairs until everyone has had a chance to connect with someone new.

Or you could just say . . .
"Hey Erin! Did you know Jess plays piano, too?"

Whatever this looks like for you, give it a try this week. Help your few connect with each other. **Connect them with someone new.**

And remember, if you want your small group conversations to matter more, you might want to try this before the conversation begins: **connect with them** and help them **connect with each other.**

Because before a kid can connect with God, they may need to connect with someone who's connected with God.

QUIZ:

HOW WELL DO YOU CONNECT WITH YOUR FEW?

Group time has started and it's up to you to get the conversation going on the right foot! Before you can go deeper, it's probably a good idea to connect with your few. Answer the questions below to see how well you CONNECT with your few each week.

What's the best way you've found to check in with your few and their families during the week?

Do you make it a priority to connect with each of your kids and greet them before small group begins?

QUIZ

Do the kids in your group usually connect with each other before small group begins?

🖊

....

....

....

....

....

What's your go-to icebreaker question? (You know, other than, "How was your week?")

🖊

....

....

....

....

....

QUIZ

What was the last thing that made your whole group laugh? Like really hard?

What was the last thing that made your whole group laugh? Like really hard?

🖊

If we picked a random name from your small group roster, could you tell us three things about that kid?

🖊

When new kids join or visit your group, how do you help them feel comfortable and connected?

🖊

3

chapter three
know

Know

(Talk about YOURSELVES)

So let's say you've . . .
prepared for your small group conversation.
connected with your few.
helped your few connect with each other.

Now—finally—you can start having a conversation about faith.

Right?

Well . . .
Almost.
Hang in there for just a few more minutes.

There's one more thing you should probably do before you have a conversation with your few about faith.

But first, imagine this.

You're in line at the grocery store. You get to the front of the line and the cashier greets you with a big smile. As he scans your frozen pizza, he asks, "Would you rather battle one horse-sized hamster or one hundred hamster-sized horses?" You blink a few times. Then you stammer something about the hamster and he says, "Now what's the biggest spiritual battle you've ever faced?"

Kind of weird, right?

Or let's say you're on a run. You've just hit your stride when another runner you've never seen before appears at your side. She looks concerned. You take out an earbud. She introduces herself and asks, "Have you been demonstrating sexual integrity this week?"

Feeling uncomfortable yet?

You should be,
because that's creepy.

But while those questions from a stranger might leave you looking for the nearest exit, they're perfectly acceptable in the context of a small group.

Why?

Maybe because, in a small group, those questions aren't being asked by total strangers.
They're being discussed in the context of relationships.

Think about it. Who was the last person you had an
honest
open
meaningful
conversation with?

It probably wasn't your grocery store cashier or a stranger on the bike path. More than likely, it was your best friend, your mom, your spouse, or your mentor. You know—someone you trust. Someone who loves you. Someone who knows you.

Kids are no different. Sure, they may be more open than teenagers, but they have to know they're in a safe place before they can have honest conversations about big things—like faith, for example. And they probably wouldn't want to talk to that weird cashier either.

Kids won't always have honest conversations with *anyone*.
But they will have them with safe people.
They won't have honest conversations *anytime* or
anywhere.
But they will have them in safe places.

So if you want to have better small group conversations,
make sure your small group feels like a safe place. And
if you want your small group to feel like a safe place,
make sure your small group conversations don't feel like
conversations with strangers. Make sure your small group is
a place where your few feel *known*.

But here's the thing about being known.
(It might sound obvious, but stay with me.)

A kid won't *feel* known until someone knows them.

Think about this for a second—why would a kid, or you for
that matter, feel known by someone who didn't take the
time to get to know them? They wouldn't!

If you want the kids in your group to feel known,
you can't force it
and you can't fake it.
The only way to help a kid feel known
is to **actually know them.**

That's why, as an SGL, it's your job to
know the kids in your group
and help them know each other.

Knowing—really knowing—your small group is a big deal.

Because **before a kid can KNOW God loves them, they
may need to be KNOWN by *people* who know God.**

3.1

If you want your small group conversations to matter more,

know them

Know them

It's not enough to only **connect** with the kids in your group. You've got to really **know** them. And I don't just mean your favorite kids. (Yes we know you have favorites.) If you want your small group conversations to matter more, you've got to know *every kid*.

When you know a kid, you'll know . . .
their name.
their birthday.
their family.
their talents.
their fears.
their hopes.
their favorite pizza toppings.

When you know a kid, you'll know about . . .
their week.
their friends.
their spelling test on Monday.
their game on Friday.
their pet fish.
their new favorite song.
their most embarrassing moment.

Maybe that seems like a lot of things to know about every kid in your group.
I'm not saying you need to know
everything that happens
every week
to every kid.
(That would be weird. And impossible.)

I'm just saying that if you want your few to feel known in your small group, you're going to need to know them.

Here are a few ways to KNOW your few . . .

1. KNOW THEIR WORLDS

Remember when we talked about how to PREPARE for your small group conversation? One of the ways we suggested preparing for your conversation was to **consider what's happening in their lives right now.**

It makes sense, right? There are certain things that would be helpful to know before your small group conversation begins.

Before you ask what they're doing this weekend, it would be good to know Friday is Gabrielle's birthday.

Before you begin a discussion about math class, you might want to know that Katie isn't doing so well in fourth grade math.

Before you lead a conversation about trusting God, you should probably know that Jake's dad just left.

The more you know about a kid's world before your small group conversation begins, the better your conversation will be. When you know what's happening in their world, you'll be more likely to know . . .
what to say.
what not to say.
when to celebrate them.
when to challenge them.
when to comfort them.

**SMALL GROUP SURVIVAL KIT:
NOISEMAKER**
When you know your few, you know when
they need to be celebrated. But it's not
exactly easy to keep track of everything
that's happening in their lives. That's why
it's helpful to keep a noisemaker on hand.
Because whether it's because of a birthday,
a report card, a great game, or a new record
time in Mario Kart, sometimes one of your
few will need to be celebrated—and you'll
need to be prepared.

You don't need to know everything about your kids' lives
before you begin a small group conversation. The truth is
that a good small group conversation will probably teach
you something new about your few. But you shouldn't have
to wait for your small group time to catch up on their lives.

So don't.

If you want to know about their worlds . . .
watch their body language
ask them what they've seen recently
ask how they're doing.
follow up on their prayer requests.
talk with their parents.

If you want your small group conversations to matter more,
it's not enough for you to simply **CONNECT** with your few
each week. You've got to **KNOW** them—really know them.
And you can start by **knowing their worlds.**

2. KNOW THEIR PERSONALITIES

This may be a wild guess.
We could be completely wrong.

But we're going to assume that your small group is filled

with several different types of personalities.

We're also going to assume that managing all of those personalities can sometimes be a challenge. Especially when you're trying to lead a small group conversation.

Some kids dominate the conversation
and some will sit quietly.

Some are silly
and some are serious.

Some are outgoing
and some are reserved.

Some will follow the group
while some will try to lead it.

It won't always be easy to have a conversation with so many competing personalities, but here are a few tips that might help:

KNOW YOUR EXTROVERTS

They're loud. They have a lot to say. They like being the center of attention. On a good day, the extroverts in your group probably fill the room with energy, keep the conversation moving, and get everyone laughing. But on a bad day, they leave you with ringing ears, a hoarse voice, and a desperate need for a nap. But no matter what kind of day you have this week, here are a few tips for leading an extrovert in a small group conversation.

- **Be patient with them.** Remember, your few are not adults—they're kids! They're still learning to be self-aware and emotionally intelligent. In the meantime, if they're too loud, if they interrupt you too often, or if they've been talking for longer than you'd like, be patient. If you correct them, correct them with kindness (and maybe even a little humor). If you can treat them with patience, grace, and dignity, they'll be much more likely to use their energy and words for the good of your conversation next time.

- **Hear them.** After they've said what must be their 500,000th word of the day, it's not easy to give them your attention. But keep this in mind: if you can give them the focused attention they need for at least a few minutes, they'll be more likely to focus and less likely to continue seeking that attention for the rest of your conversation.
- **Sit near them.** You know who the talkers and conversation starters are in your small group. We always suggest sitting them right next to you. This way when they start rambling on and on and begin to converse about how they picked the color on their bedroom walls, you can simply put your hand on their back and say, "It's time for someone else to talk now."

SMALL GROUP SURVIVAL KIT: STRESS BALL

Have you ever led a conversation where everyone had something to say? About everything? At the exact same time? In those moments, you need a stress ball (and maybe some ear plugs). Here's how to use it—you know, besides the obvious way:

1. Clear your throat dramatically.
2. Say, "For the rest of small group, you may only speak if you are holding this ball."
3. If they follow your instructions, promise to bring them a surprise next week.
4. Ask your children's pastor for $5.00. Then buy cupcakes.

KNOW YOUR INTROVERTS

They're quiet. They're reserved. They sometimes observe your conversations more than they participate (especially if you have a few extroverts in your group). Your introverts won't be the first to respond to a small group question, but when you can get them to speak, you'll be glad they did. A small group conversation can be an intimidating environment for an introvert, so here are a few tips for keeping them involved . . .

- **Don't forget them.** It's pretty easy to favor your extroverts during a small group conversation. It makes sense. They're always ready to answer—even if their answer isn't very well thought out. But don't forget about your introverts! They may not be as vocal, but it's not because they're not processing the conversation. In fact, they're probably thinking more deeply about your conversation than your extroverts. So in your next small group conversation, don't let yourself be distracted by your extroverts. Pay attention to your introverts. They have a lot to contribute!
- **Don't surprise them.** Introverts don't usually like to be put on the spot. There are few things more uncomfortable for an introvert than being asked to speak in front of a group unexpectedly. So if you want them to participate, give a heads up. Say something like, "Hey Courtney, after this, you've got the next question." Or try, "I'd love to hear what you think about this, but I'll tell you what I think first." You might even want to try slipping her the questions in advance so she can think about her responses before the conversation begins.
- **Don't force them.** As you get to know your introverts, you'll begin to learn when to push them to speak and when to let them sit back and observe. As an SGL, you'll figure out when to challenge your few without making them feel pressured, uncomfortable, or embarrassed.

It's not easy to lead a group filled with competing personalities, but you can do it! The more you know your few, the better you'll be at managing the conversation.

If you want to make your small group conversations matter more, you'll need to **KNOW** your few. And you can do that by **knowing their personalities.**

SMALL GROUP SURVIVAL KIT: DECK OF CARDS
Sometimes you need to shift the balance of power between your extroverts and introverts. A great tip we got from a fellow small group leader was to always bring a deck of cards to group—regular cards, *Uno* cards, *Candyland* cards—any cards will work. Hand them out at the beginning of your group time and when it comes to answering questions you can call on all the "blues" or all the "6s" to answer the next question. Now you've got a reason to let everyone have an equal chance at sharing during group!

3. KNOW THEIR DISTRACTIONS

When my (Afton) few were in first grade, I had a few boys that loved to bring their Legos to group. At first, I thought it was a great thing to connect with them over—I'd ask what they were building and what world it came from and how long it took to build them. I loved having a tool to connect over and they loved telling me about their creations. But the thing about Legos is . . . one normal-sized thing can turn into 100 tiny things. And before I knew it, my whole group had several Lego bricks each that they then could turn into whatever they wanted, fight over, and throw. And no matter how much I asked for them to stay in pockets or gave them our own "on activity" craft items, those Legos would forever be everywhere.

So a few weeks in, after I *oohed* and *aahed* over their
newest Lego Star Wars ship or Lord of the Rings tower, I
asked if I could place them in the toy bag, so they would
be safe during group time, and we could take them back
out at the end.

I know, I know. You're probably thinking I should have . . .
taken charge.
talked to them about respect.
threatened to call their moms.

And maybe you're right.
But you know what?
Sometimes it's just easier to hide the toys.

SMALL GROUP SURVIVAL KIT: ZIPPER STORAGE BAG

There are few things more distracting than a
toy brought from home during a small group
conversation with kids. Or a marker being
dissected. Or a football from home. Or a
bracelet slowly falling apart on the floor. If
you've ever had to pause a conversation
because someone was poking, playing,
piecing, or throwing some things you might
want to keep a large zipper storage bag
handy. On the weeks you don't want to fight
a battle against their distractions, start your
small group by asking everyone to drop their
toys, permanent markets, or maybe even their
phones into the bag (yours, too!) until your
conversation is over.

I don't know what the distractions are for your small
groups.
Maybe it's markers.
Or their toys from home.
Or the group sitting nearby.
Or everyone taking fifteen separate trips to the bathroom.

Whatever it is for your few, as their SGL, you might
want to know what distracts them from your small group
conversation. Because when you know what distracts them,
you can help eliminate those distractions *before* they derail
your conversation.

If you want to make your small group conversations matter
more, you'll need to **KNOW** your few. When you know
their worlds, know their personalities and know their
distractions, you'll be better equipped to lead your small
group conversations.

Because if you want this week's small group conversation
to matter more, your few need to feel known by you.
KNOW THEM.

3.2

If you want your small group conversations to matter more, help them

know
each
other

Know each other

You already know how important it is for you to know your few. But just like how you need to help your few connect with each other, you're not the only person your few need to be *known* by. They need to know, and be known by, each other.

Just like the people in ancient times developed their view of God as . . .
the God of Abraham
the God of Isaac
or the God of Moses,

you have developed a sense of who God is because you have met . . .
the God of Talia
the God of Amanda
or the God of Jeff.

Here's the point. God has always used people to demonstrate His story of redemption.

It was true then. And it's true today.
It was true for you. And it's true for your few.

So if you want a kid to know God, maybe one of the most important things you can do is to give them a community of people who will talk with them, hang out with them, and do life with them. People who know God and who know them.

You're one of those people.
But you're not the only person they need.
They need to know (and be known by) you.
But they need to know (and be known by) the rest of their small group too.

So make sure you know your few. Then help them know each other.

Here are a few ways to do that . . .

1. MAKE GROUP MEMORIES

If you want to move your few
from casually **connecting** with each other
to really **knowing** each other,
you might want to consider making some memories together.

When you make memories together outside of small group, you'll help your few know each other in a deeper way. And as they get to know one another better, they'll begin to have better conversations.

So see a movie.
Go apple-picking.
Bake cookies.
Ride a roller coaster.
Sing really loud to their favorite song.

And when you're together in small group, take time to talk about your memories. Then make plans to make new ones. So help your few know each other. **Make group memories** together.

You know during Large Group when the host will ask for small group leader volunteers to come onstage and play a game or participate in some way? Do all your kids frantically raise your arms, hoping and pleading that you'll be the one to go up this time to endure some sort of embarrassment or win the group loads of candy? Mine (Afton) do. And one Sunday, it worked. I couldn't tell you what the main idea of this particular week was, but I can tell you that it must've had something to do with perseverance. Because as I sat in a chair onstage, the host of the game proceeded to create a work of art with my hair—filled with pipe-cleaners, purple hair spray, scrunchies, and . . . *glitter*. When the host finished their masterpiece, they asked me if I had any plans today and I answered, amid quite a bit of laughter, "A baby shower."

My few thought this was the funniest thing they've ever heard. They laughed the rest of the group time over my hair, and to this day—three years later—someone will jokingly mention, "Remember that time you had to go to a *BABY SHOWER!*" Some of the best group memories are made when we can throw off any embarrassment, pour glitter on our heads, and *laugh* with our few.

2. BUILD GROUP IDENTITY

We are wired for community.
We want a place to belong.
A group.
A family.
A tribe.
If you don't believe me, go to a football game sometime. The team colors. The face paint. The screaming. Now those people are passionate about their tribes.

Your few are no different. Okay, they probably don't paint their faces and scream during small group (or maybe they do), but it's still true. The kids in your small group want a place to belong. They want a tribe, a family, and a group they can call their own.

If you want your small group to really know each other,
help them see themselves as a group.

How? Well, you could try . . .
creating a group name.
inviting them over to play games.
making matching T-shirts.
inventing a new small group tradition.
having an inside joke.

Because when your group has a strong sense of group
identity, they'll feel like they belong. And when they feel
like they belong, they'll be more likely to open up in
conversation. So help your few know each other. Build a
group identity together.

3. SET GROUP GUIDELINES

If you want your few to *know* each other, making memories
and building a group identity will help. But if you want your
few to *really* know each other, they need to feel safe. Safe
enough to be . . .
real.
vulnerable.
honest.

That's where confidentiality comes in. Confidentiality isn't
exactly easy to monitor. You typically won't know about a
breach until after—
Susan has told the whole Girl Scout troup about Rosa's
phobia of clowns.
Tiffany has told Jose about Robyn's crush on him.
Jace has shown the whole class pictures of Nick's blankie.

We would all love to have the perfect group filled with
enough respect and maturity to know for sure that what is
said in group stays in group. In fact, that should probably
be a rule you set up in the beginning. Absolute, one
hundred percent, swear on my stash of Halloween candy

confidentiality should always be your goal. But we have to be realistic.

You probably won't be able to prevent every breach in confidentiality, but you can challenge your few to set guidelines that will help your small group feel safe.

And since they're kids, it's probably a good idea to let them be part of the guideline-setting process.

You might want to ask them, especially when it comes to sensitive subjects . . .
What should we promise to always do?
What should we promise to never do?
How are we going to treat each other?

Because when you set group guidelines, your few will feel safe enough to be honest in your small group conversations. And honesty is a crucial part of getting to know each other. So **help your few know each other. Set group guidelines together.**

If you want your small group conversations to matter more, you might want to make this part of your weekly conversation: **know them** and **help them know each other.**

Because before a kid can know God, they may need to be known by someone who knows God.

QUIZ:

HOW WELL DO YOU KNOW YOUR FEW?

Shopkins or My Little Pony? Soccer or football? Dance or gymnastics? Answer the questions below to see how well you KNOW your few.

How well do your few know each other? Do they know each other's names? Birthdays? Favorite pizza toppings?

Which of your few do you know the least?

QUIZ

Make a list of your favorite small group memories.

QUIZ

How comfortable are your few with being open and honest during your small group conversations?

Do you consider your few to be your friends? Your best friends? (Because that might be going a little bit too far.)

4

chapter
four
engage

Engage

(talk about the TRUTH)

Okay.
Finally.
This is the part you've been waiting for.

Now that you've . . .
prepared for your small group conversation
connected as a group
and gotten to **know** each other
. . . you're ready to actually **engage** your small group in a
conversation.

But not just any conversation.
A really important conversation.
A conversation about authentic faith.

After all, that's why you became an SGL in the first place,
isn't it? So you could lead kids in conversations about
truths that will shape their faith and future.

Sure, it's taken us some time to get here, but that was
intentional. Before we could talk about building authentic
faith in your small group, we had to talk about building
authentic relationships first.

When you take the time to invest relationally in your few by
. . .
connecting with them
helping them connect with each other
knowing them
helping them know each other

. . . you lay a foundation of trust, influence, and relationships that you're going to need if you want your few to ultimately engage in a conversation about faith.

But before we go any further, let's clarify something.

Let's talk about that word **ENGAGE**.

Maybe we could have called this chapter **TALK**.
Or **DISCUSS**.
Or **PARTICIPATE**.
Although talking, discussing, and participating are *some* of the things you probably hope your small group will do, those words don't quite capture the goal of a small group conversation. Not completely.

You see, when you're finally ready to begin a conversation about authentic faith with your small group, your goal isn't for them to simply talk, or discuss, or *participate* in your conversation.

When your few participate in a conversation, they might . . .
listen.
respond.
be respectful.
summarize.

But when they *engage* in a conversation, they'll do more than participate. They will . . .
think.
share.
question.
discuss.
debate.
own.
personalize.

It's pretty easy to get your small group to participate in a conversation. All you need is the right combination of stern looks, candy bribes, and threats to call their parents.

But with kids, engagement is a little trickier—at least, when you're talking about faith. If you're discussing Taylor Swift or puppies, engaging kids in a conversation is simple. But when you're not talking about Taylor Swift or puppies— when you're talking about doubt or forgiveness or prayer or courage—how do you move your few beyond simply *participating* in the conversation?

How do you **ENGAGE** them in a conversation about authentic faith?

Learning to engage your few in your conversations won't always be easy. You won't always get it right. It won't always come naturally. But no matter how your small group conversation went *last* week, there is always something you can do to better engage your few *next* week.

So if you want to better engage your few in your small group conversations, there are a few things you'll probably need to do *less*. You may need to . . .
talk less.
control less.
script less.

And there are a few things you'll probably need to do *more*. Like . . .
listen more.
lead more.
improvise more.

As you work to better engage your few in conversations about faith, there will still be weeks when you'll feel frustrated. There will be weeks when you'll wish you'd said or done or handled things differently. There will be weeks when you'll wonder if you're really cut out for this small-group-leading thing.

We know. We've been there.

Leading a small group can be difficult. And trying to engage a group of kids in a conversation about authentic faith might be the most difficult part. (That and making sure they don't break a bone during group time.)

So on the weeks when it's difficult to engage your few in a faith conversation, it wouldn't hurt to remember this.

Your few won't remember every small group conversation you'll ever have.
But they will remember more than you think.

Even on the weeks when you're sure they weren't engaged in your conversation, **what gets said in small group probably has more of an impact than you think it does.** The words your few share in small group may seem like small things, but they have tremendous influence.

Remember what we said earlier? **Your small group conversations matter**—maybe more than you think. But with the right amount of preparation, relationships, technique, and patience, you can make **your small group conversations matter even more.**

So if you want to make your small group conversations matter more (and we know you do), then you might want to be more intentional about how you engage your few during your conversations about faith.

Because **before a kid can ENGAGE in a life of authentic faith, they may need you to ENGAGE them in a conversation about authentic faith.**

And here are three ways to do just that.

When my (Afton) few were in kindergarten, I left about half the time wondering if I had even gotten any meaningful

words across other than "Here's how you hold the
scissors," or, "Let's only make a paper airplane out of one
of your activity pages." I'd leave wondering . . . did I say
anything meaningful? Did I say something about faith? Did
I lead them to understand how what we're talking about
today impacts their lives tomorrow?

Now, almost four years later, my group has some of the
most consistent kids that have come back year after year,
week after week. I've seen them onstage playing orphans
in *Annie*, and even seen a few take their next steps in faith
through baptism. So even when you leave your small group
time wondering if that conversation mattered, remember
that it did, because creating a place where kids feel safe
to start having faith conversations is the best thing you
can do.

4.1

If you want your small group conversations to matter more,

speak less, listen more.

(Let's talk about you.)

speak less, listen more

We may not know you, but if you're leading a small group of kids, we're going to guess you took this job because . . .
you love God.
you love kids.
you want to tell kids about God.

Us too!

But trying to *tell* kids everything you know about God probably isn't the most effective way to influence their faith. If simply *telling* kids what to believe led to a more authentic faith, we wouldn't even need small groups. We could just preach longer sermons.

You know better, though.
You know the power of a small group.
You know the importance of a community.
And you know the impact you can have on a kid's faith through conversation.

See, the goal is to try to get kids to get together and work on something. Your goal isn't for kids to have a classroom debate like they will in college, but the goal is to try to get them to have a conversation. Have you ever listened to kids talk to each other? It's fascinating to listen to them share what's going on in their heads and their hearts! We know that kids learn best in a hands-on, collaborative environment way more than they do in lecture.

Maybe that's because of how kid's brains are developing during this phase.
Or because they're learning to understand multiple points of view.
Or because they tend to trust their peers more than they trust adults.
Or because they're occasionally skeptical of authority figures.
Or because they often process ideas better when they talk about them out loud.

Or maybe it's because of all these things.

Whatever the reasons, it's true. Whether the topic is reading, science, or the Great Commandment, kids will learn best when they can . . .
talk about it.
ask questions.
share their opinions.
find answers together.

But, sometimes, we SGLs forget about that. (Or maybe we never learned it in the first place.) Sometimes, we want to be the person who . . .
talks about it.
asks the questions.
shares our opinions.
has all the answers.

When I (Adam) started as a small group leader, the only thing I could think of was getting to the stage. I wanted to be a storyteller so bad I could taste it! So, it finally happened. But the problem was, when I got up there and started telling stories, the only thing I could think was, "Yes, this is cool . . . but it only matters if they remember and apply it when they get to small group." I learned very quickly it was all about the small group leader and not about what anyone did on stage. An onstage performer's moment lasts for a moment, but the influence of an SGL lasts for a lifetime.

Because, you see, you're not a teacher. You're a small group leader. And as an SGL, yes, you'll need to talk sometimes. But more importantly, you'll need to listen.

In fact, we'd recommend sticking with The 80/20 Rule. In every small group conversation, you should spend at least 80 percent of your time *listening,* and only 20 percent of your time *talking.*

That's what we mean by **speaking less** and **listening more.**

Okay, we know. The 80/20 rule might seem like an unrealistic goal. Depending on the age of the kids you lead, maybe it is. If that's the case, make it The 60/40 rule! The principle is still the same: speak less, and listen more.

Here's the thing, though. Even when we *try* to be better listeners, we're usually not very good at it. In fact, when one of your few is speaking, you will probably only pay attention to 48% of what she says. And of the 48% that you hear, you'll only remember 50% of it. It's not just you, though. We're all far worse listeners than we probably think we are.

But if you want to engage your few in a better small group conversation, you'll need to become a better conversationalist. And that starts with being a good listener. And being a good listener takes practice. So here are four steps you can take to **speak less and listen more.**

1. LOOK

Now, this might sound obvious, but stick with us. When one of the kids in your small group is speaking, **look at them.**

(I told you it might sound obvious.)

But if we're honest, we'd probably all agree that making eye contact during a conversation isn't always easy or natural. (Especially when there are so many interesting things happening on your phone.)
Or when you can't remember which question you're supposed to ask next.
Or when the group to your left decided to do their moving activity during your look-it-up in the Bible activity..

Making eye contact with your few isn't always easy (especially in a small group setting), but it's a big deal.

When you **look** at your few as they speak, you communicate that what they say matters. And if they believe what they say matters, they'll be a lot more likely to keep talking. So put the phone down, limit any distractions you might have, and **look** when they're speaking.

2. FOCUS

Looking at your few when they're talking is a great step toward becoming a better listener, but it's only the first step. If a kid in your group is talking and you're busy . . . rehearsing what you'll say next
wondering if you could pull off her same outfit
silently singing your favorite Justin Timberlake song
. . . then it doesn't matter how well you've maintained eye contact. Your listening skills still need some work.

We have a friend named Heather. Heather is one of the best listeners we know. That's why, when Heather told us she had a trick for becoming a better listener, we knew we had to . . . well, listen. Heather said that when one of her few is speaking, asking a question, or telling a story, Heather imagines she's wearing a set of blinders. (When Heather told us this, she actually put her hands on either side of her face, just in case we didn't get the picture.)

Those imaginary blinders, she said, are a reminder to stay focused on the kid in front of her, no matter what. Even if someone tries to interrupt, or her phone vibrates, or she gets hit in the back of the head with a dodgeball, Heather is committed to staying focused on the kid in front of her.

The second step to becoming a better listener is to **focus on what they're saying.**

3. SUMMARIZE

Once you've mastered the art of looking and focusing while one of the kids in your group is speaking, it's time to take your listening skills one step further. Once you've heard what they've said, take a second to **summarize what you heard.**

We've already said that we're not always the best listeners. But kids aren't exactly the best communicators either. They can be . . .
long-winded.
hasty.
vague.
random.
(Okay, let's face it—so can we.) Your kids might even tell stories so long that, when it ends, no one can remember why they were telling it in the first place. That's why summarizing is so important. When you summarize what your few have said, you help the conversation move forward.

You might say . . .

"So to summarize, _____."
"In other words, _____."
"So you're saying _____."

When you summarize what you've heard, you . . .
let them know you were listening.

make sure you understand.
help clarify their thoughts for the rest of the group.

The third step to becoming a better listener is to
summarize.

4. ASK

After you've summarized what one of your few has said,
don't move on until you've **asked** them this question:
"Did I get that right?" Because the reality is, no matter
how great you are at listening to a kid, you will sometimes
misunderstand what they're trying to say.

So when you've summarized what they said, ask if you
understood them. There are two ways they could respond.

1. **They could correct you.** If they do, that's great! It
    means you're getting clarity.
2. **They could agree with you.** That *might* be good. If
    they agree with how you've summarized what they've
    said, it might mean that you got it right. *Or* . . . it
    might mean you've misunderstood them, but they're
    uncomfortable correcting you. That's why knowing
    your few is so important. The more you know them,
    the more likely you'll be to discern when they're being
    open and when they're holding back.

So before you move on to the next question, **ask if you
understood them.**

If you want to make your small group conversations
matter more, you'll need to **ENGAGE** your few in those
conversations. But you might want to start by becoming a
better listener. So when your few open up, don't forget to
look, focus, summarize, and ask. That's what it means to
speak less and listen more.

QUIZ:

HOW WELL DO YOU LISTEN TO YOUR FEW?

Have you ever heard of active listening? It's a GREAT tool for small group leaders. The basic idea is that you are ENGAGED as someone is telling you a story or something about themselves. Here's a few questions you should ask yourself to see if you're a good listener.

When someone in your group is talking, how often do you try to finish their ~~sandwiches~~ sentences?

🖊

When you're telling a story, what are some signs that your few have definitely stopped listening?

🖊

QUIZ

When one of your few is telling a story, what are some things that make it difficult to stay focused?

What percent of your small group conversations do you usually spend speaking?

What's one thing you're going to do to become a better listener?

4.2

If you want your small group conversations to matter more,

control less, lead more.

(Let's talk about your questions.)

control less, lead more

When you're preparing to lead a small group conversation, it's usually a good idea to **think with the end in mind.** Thinking with the end in mind means deciding where you want your small group conversation to go. When you identify a destination before your conversation begins, you'll be a lot more likely to actually get there.

After all, you're the small group leader. So if you're going to lead a conversation with your few, you should probably know where you're leading them.

So what is your destination exactly? Well, this changes every week.

If your children's pastor sends you a weekly email, your destination might already be determined for you. To find out, open your weekly email (if you've got one) and look for a summary of that week's activities and conversation. If you're really lucky, your children's pastor may have even summarized the topic into a catchy bottom line, like . . .
Remember God is with you.
Make the wise choice.
Be the friend you want to have.

That summary, or bottom line, is your children's pastor's destination. It's what they'll be teaching. It's the one idea they hope the kids in your ministry will learn and remember all week long.

But that's not *your* destination.
Well . . . okay, it's *almost* your destination.
But not exactly.

You see, if you were **teaching** kids, your destination would be to help them **learn** or **remember** what you've taught.

But you're not a teacher. You're a small group leader. So your destination isn't *just* to help them learn or remember what they've heard from stage. Your destination is to help your few **personalize** and **apply** what they've heard.

Let's say the storyteller is teaching, "Make the wise choice." Then your destination for your small group conversation might be to help your few identify one thing they can do to start making wiser choices.

If your storyteller is teaching, "Remember God is with you," your destination might be to challenge your few to consider how their lives might be different if they really believed God was with them.

See the difference?

In small group, your destination isn't **knowledge**. That's what the teaching is for.
In small group, your destination is **application**. That's what your conversation is for.

So you've got your destination in mind. Great.
Now you've just got to get your group
from where they are
to where you want them to go.

Easy, right?

(If you answered yes, we're not convinced you've ever met

a kid before. The only place it's easy to get a kid to go is a pizza place.)

So how do you get your few to your destination? We're so glad you asked!

You have two options.
You can control them (or try, at least).
Or you can lead them somewhere.

Some SGLs make the mistake of trying to control their small group conversations. They know where they're going. They know how to get there. They have a map. They have a schedule. They're going to make sure their few get to their destination *no matter what*. And they're definitely not going to sightsee or stop for Doritos on the way.

That approach is probably helpful if you're trying to get to a dentist appointment on time, but it's not the best way to approach your small group conversations.

When you try to **control** your small group conversation . . .
it's difficult to adjust or improvise.
your way is the right way.
your questions usually have right answers.
you discourage disagreement.
you demand respect.
your few follow you . . . but not willingly.

But there's a second way to approach your small group conversations.

SGLs who have learned how to lead a small group conversation, rather than control it, still know where they're headed and how to get there. But they're comfortable with detours, Dorito stops, and taking the scenic route. They know not everyone will arrive at their destination at the same time and, sometimes, they understand they'll need to change their destination completely. But no matter where they're headed, they're committed to leading their few toward their destination (even if it takes a little longer to get there than they had originally planned).

When you **lead** your few in a small group conversation . . .
you can manage rabbit trails.
you admit you don't have all the answers.
your questions are open-ended.
you encourage discussion and debate.
you value their opinions and ideas.
your few follow you willingly.

As an SGL, we understand the temptation to want to control your few. With so much at stake, it makes sense. But here's the bad news. You can't actually control your few. So when you control less and lead more, you recognize that, while you can't **control** your few, you can still **lead** them.

But, maybe all this talk about detours and Doritos has made you a little uneasy. Maybe you're wondering how, exactly, to lead a small group conversation without controlling it.

We're so glad you asked.

It's not always easy to give up control. But if you want to engage your few in a better small group conversation, you'll need to become a better leader—not a controller— of your small group conversations. And that starts with the kinds of questions you ask. So here are three things you can do to **control less and lead more.**

1. ASK BETTER QUESTIONS

In case no one has told you this already, let us be the ones to break it to you.

As an SGL, your job is not to be an answer-giver.
Your job is to be a question-asker.

That's a relief, right? You don't actually have to give correct answers to every question a kid asks, as though you were some brilliant walking, talking biblical encyclopedia. If the job of a small group leader was to have all the right answers, your volunteer application process probably should have been a lot more difficult.

If it hasn't happened already, one of your few will eventually ask you a difficult question. If you don't have a perfect answer, it's okay to say, "I don't know."

But since your job is to be a question-asker, here's an even better idea. Even if you *do* have the perfect answer to that tricky question, don't give an answer. Instead, ask more questions.

As a small group leader, questions are your most important tool. A good question can help you . . .
learn about your few.
understand their perspectives.
make them think.
take them on a journey.

And a good question will help the kids in your small group . . .
clarify their beliefs.
reconsider their perspectives.
change their opinions.
identify a next step.

So, since the questions you ask are such an important tool, let's talk about how to ask the right ones—questions that don't *control* your few, but *lead* them somewhere.

Questions that *control* are questions whose answers are often . . .

one word
fact-based
yes-or-no
right-or-wrong.

They're questions like . . .
Did you like the talk this week?
Is lying a sin?
Who was the apostle Paul?
Don't you agree that . . . ?

But then there are *better* questions—questions that lead your few toward your destination, but don't control their journey.

These questions don't ask for answers. They invite responses. These questions . . .
are open-ended.
are opinion-based.
invite feedback.
don't have a right answer.

They're questions like . . .
Have you ever . . . ?
What do you think about . . . ?
What do you think would happen if . . . ?
What's one thing you can do this week to . . . ?

In a small group conversation, the best kinds of questions are questions that ask your few to share their experiences, their opinions, their observations, and their ideas. They're questions that expect disagreement and encourage discussion. And they're questions that invite your few to think, debate, and come to conclusions together. That's what it looks like for your few to engage in a conversation, instead of just participate.

So if you want to better engage your few by controlling less and leading more, start by asking better questions.

2. VALUE SILENCE

This may be difficult to believe, but it's true. Silence in
a small group conversation can actually be your friend.
Seriously! Sometimes, a little silence is exactly what
you need.

Okay, I know. Silence in a small group can be awkward—
and might even seem unattainable if you've got a group of
talkers. If you ask a question and no one responds within
three seconds, you might sometimes go into a mental
tailspin.
Was that a stupid question?
Did it even make sense?
Why aren't they talking?
They're never going to talk.
This is a disaster.
Do they all hate me?

Sure, sometimes your group will be silent because you
asked a dumb question. But most of the time, your
question was probably just fine.

Don't rush to fill the silence with an answer or a quick
change of subject. If you can get comfortable with silence,
you can use it. Let them . . .
sit.
think.
process.

And while you wait . . .
gather your thoughts.
watch their body language.
check the clock.

When silence sets in, time moves slowly. Ten seconds might
feel like five minutes—especially if you're uncomfortable.
Chances are, your few are just as uncomfortable with
the silence as you are. If you can be patient, someone

will break the silence. After you ask the question, give them thirty seconds to respond. If no one has spoken up after thirty seconds, then you might want to think about rephrasing your question. But before you dive in to rescue them from the silence, give it time.

In the meantime, look around. If you pay attention, you might even learn something during those thirty seconds of unspeakable torture. Do they look like they're thinking? That's a good thing! Do they look confused? You may need to reword your question. Are they all avoiding eye contact? The question may be too personal. Are they smirking or glancing nervously at each other? You may have uncovered a topic they talk about outside of small group, but are embarrassed to talk about inside of small group.

Leading a small group conversation isn't easy when you feel like you're getting the silent treatment. But if you want to better engage your few in conversation by controlling less and leading more, learn to **value silence.**

3. UNDER-REACT

Sometimes it's the silence of your few that causes you stress. Other times, one of your few will say something so shocking you'd happily trade it for an entire day of awkward silence.

Because, you see, controlling less and leading more can be risky.

When you . . .
ask questions that are open-ended
welcome their opinions and feedback
encourage discussion and debate
. . . you won't always be able to anticipate what they'll say.

And if your small group is a place where your few feel safe enough to be honest, your questions might actually prompt

someone to be honest.
Honest about what they think.
Honest about what they believe.
Honest about what they've done.

When one of your few says something in group that
surprises you, you might feel like you've lost control.

You haven't.

Take a breath.
Freak out on the inside.
Thank them for sharing.
And ask more questions.

There was a Sunday that I (Adam) got called in to be a
substitute small group leader for a fourth grade group.
After the Bible story, I asked the kids some questions and
then opened it up for anyone to ask a question. One of
the boys raised his hand and asked, "Mr. Adam, my mom
and dad live together and won't get married. Do you know
why?" I obviously responded with, "That's an interesting
question. You should ask your small group leader when
he's back next week." I'm kidding. On the inside I started
to feel panicky. I never could've prepared for this question
to be asked! But on the outside, I remained calm and
interested. "That's an interesting question. How does that
situation make you feel?"

And I (Afton) once had a first grader in my group casually
mention that her "uncle killed a snake last week and put
it in his freezer." The facial expressions I suppressed that
day should have won an award. Working with kids, a lot
of times they'll tell us things that are silly or way too much
information. But when we under-react to the stories they
tell us—no matter how silly or weird—we're communicating
that this is a place where anything can be shared, because
our group is a safe place to talk about anything.

But when one of your few shares something shocking, there's one question you should never ask: *Why?*
Why do you think that?
Why don't you believe that?
Why did you do that?

Asking *why* might feel like a reflex. It will be on the tip of your tongue. When a kid confesses something that shocks you, *why* will seem like the right thing to ask.

But don't.

When you ask *why*—especially immediately after a kid has opened up to you—you will lose your opportunity to have a conversation. And without a conversation, you will lose your opportunity to lead them somewhere new.

That's because the question *why* shuts down a conversation. When we hear *why,* we feel like we're being judged. We want to defend ourselves. We want to put up walls.

That doesn't mean you shouldn't ask *any* questions. It just means you should ask different questions—questions that don't start with *why.* Like . . .

How do you feel about what has happened?
What led you to this decision?
How do you think your parents might feel about this?
What might happen if you did that again?
What do you think God would have to say about this?

When you decide not to ask *why,* even when you're freaking out on the inside, you invite a conversation, instead of shutting it down. When you avoid asking *why,*
you . . .
show curiosity instead of judgment.
seek to understand instead of being understood.
choose to listen instead of panic.

When you under-react instead over-react, you prove to your few that your small group really is a safe place. Because, if you want your few to engage in your small group conversation, you'll need to help them see your group is a place that is safe enough to talk about anything—even the things that shock you like how long it's been since they brushed their teeth, the thing they said to their parents, or how much money the tooth fairy leaves under their pillow.

So if you want your small group conversations to matter more, ask better questions, value silence, and under-react. And remember, you're not the small group controller. You're the small group leader. So control less, and lead more.

QUIZ:

HOW WELL DO YOU LEAD YOUR FEW?

This is what makes an SGL different than a Sunday School teacher—you've got to be a master conversationalist. Here's a few quick questions to see how well you lead your group.

When was the last time your small group time felt out of control? What happened?

Have you ever held your group hostage until you discussed every single question on your small group guide?

QUIZ

What's the best conversation your few have had recently?
What was the question that sparked that conversation?

✎

....

....

....

....

....

When was the last time your small group went silent?
How did you handle it?

✎

....

....

....

....

....

QUIZ

Next time one of your few shares something shocking, what's one thing you can do to be sure you under-react (besides practicing your best poker face in the mirror)?

4.3

If you want your small group conversations to matter more,

script less, improvise more.

(Let's talk about your plan.)

script less, improvise more

As you prepare for your small group conversation each week, you probably have an idea in mind of how the conversation will go. That's great! Having a plan is an important part of preparing for your small group conversation. But as you prepare, and rehearse, and read your small group questions in advance, keep in mind:

There is no script for a small group conversation.
At some point, things will not go according to plan.
And you will probably have to improvise.

Improvisation is key. You'll have to learn to do it as an SGL. I (Adam) remember a time a kid told me that he was going to fail his math class and his parents were going to spank him when he got home. Now, you can have whatever opinion you want on that issue, but I had to deal with it in the moment—in front of a group of kids whose families all handled discipline differently. What do you say to the rest of the group when this comes up? Sometimes you just need to be encouraging, and talk to the parents afterward. It's difficult to respond on the fly, but it's these moments that really take our groups to the next level.

I'm not saying your small group needs to form an improv comedy troupe or that you need to come to small group equipped with a prop box of pool noodles. I'm just saying that, as a small group leader, you should always be prepared for your small group conversation to not go according to plan.

There's a principle in improv comedy. It's called the "Yes, and . . ." principle. According to this principle, the best improv happens when everyone performing decides to say, "Yes, and . . ." to whatever happens next.

It starts by saying "Yes." When you say *yes*, you agree to accept whatever situation, story, or energy the rest of your group throws your way.

"Yes, I am dressed like a hot dog."
"Yes, we are on the moon."
"Yes, I am a little grumpy today."

And when you say take your "Yes" a step further by saying, "Yes, and . . ." you not only accept what's been thrown at you, but you then build on it.

Like this . . .
"Yes, I am dressed like a hot dog, and I'm also late for my doctor's appointment."
"Yes, we are on the moon and, hey, it's made of ice cream!"
"Yes, I am a little grumpy, but that's because my eyebrows are missing."

You probably will never lead a small group while on the moon or dressed like a hot dog. (But I've seen the kinds of games children's pastors play, so maybe that whole missing-your-eyebrows situation is not all that unrealistic.) But here's the point. If you want to engage your few in better conversations, you're going to need to be ready to improvise—to take whatever your few throw at you, and then build on it.

Like this . . .

Yes, there are thirty-two of you. Let's play a game to learn each other's names!

Yes, next week is Christmas and none of you are paying attention to this conversation, so let's plan a Christmas party!

Yes, that question you just asked is completely off-topic, but everyone seems interested, so let's talk about it.

Most of the time, you'll only need to improvise a little.
Like when a question isn't working.
Or your few are too fidgety.
Or too talkative.
Or you have a first-time visitor.

But other times, you may need to throw away your plan entirely.
Like when thirty-two kids show up.
Or only one girl shows up.
Or your entire group is fighting.
Or one of your few experiences a tragedy.

As SGLs who have been forced to improvise more times than we can count, we want to tell *you* something we wish someone had told *us*.

You are allowed to improvise.
In fact, you should probably plan on it.

Because if you want to engage your few in a better small group conversation, you'll need to get comfortable with being uncomfortable. And that starts by letting go of your plan, saying "Yes, and . . ." and choosing to **script less, and improvise more.**

Here are four ways to do that.

1. CHANGE THE QUESTION

You won't always be able to predict the kinds of questions that will work for your small group. Sometimes a question may take you by surprise and start a great conversation. Other times, what you thought was a great conversation starter may result in blank stares and looks of utter confusion.

Sometimes your few might have trouble responding to one of your open-ended questions. That could be because the question is confusing, or maybe it's just because they're a little tired that day. But if your few are having trouble answering an open ended question, go ahead—change the question.

Here's an example.

Let's say your few are struggling to respond to the question, "How often do you think about God?" Maybe the question was a little *too* open ended. Maybe they're not sure how to put their responses into words. If they're having difficulty, ask the question again. But this time, give them a few options to choose from like: "On a scale of 1 to 5, how often do you think about God?"

In a small group conversation, open-ended questions are usually best. But when your few are struggling to respond, turning an open-ended question into a multiple-choice question can help narrow their options.

Or maybe the problem isn't the question. Maybe your few aren't responding because their responses would be too personal or intimate or embarrassing. If that's the case, you don't need to throw away the question entirely. You just need to make it a little less personal.

So instead of saying, "Tell me about the last time you lied," you might say, "Tell me about a time someone lied to you."

Or instead of, "Which rule at your house is the hardest to keep?" you could ask, "What's one rule you've heard that would be really tough to keep?"

In a small group conversation, it's good to ask tough questions. But when a question seems a little *too* tough for your few, making the question a little less personal can get the conversation moving again.

No matter how much you plan for your small group, your small group conversation can't be scripted. That's why it's so important to improvise. So if you want to better engage your few by scripting less and improvising more, **change a question or two.** You have permission!

2. TRY AN ACTIVITY

Sometimes changing a question is all the improvisation you'll need to help your conversation get unstuck. But other times, you may need to try something a little more drastic. Okay, maybe drastic isn't the right word. We don't mean to scare you.

But on the weeks when your group is . . .
too talkative
not talkative
silly
restless
distracted
. . . you might want to move away from the lesson in your hands and try something different—like an old favorite.

Maybe you've already improvised by changing an open-ended question into a scale question, like "On a scale of 1-5, how close do you feel to God right now?" To turn that scale question into an activity, you might try this: "On a scale of *this* wall to *that* wall, stand in the place that represents how close you feel to God right now."

Or you could hand out pens and paper. Then ask your few
to write down or draw a picture of their responses to a
question or two. When they're finished writing or drawing,
you could . . .
read their responses out loud.
ask them to explain what's on their paper.
post them on a wall or bulletin board.

Or maybe you make a small group video about what you've
been learning. Ask each of your few to share what they're
learning in 30 seconds or less. Then use your phone to edit
their clips into a complete video.

Or you might decide to break up the group dynamics by
splitting into pairs. When everyone has a partner, spend
time praying together or discussing questions one at a time.

Or maybe you ask your few to work together on a
project, challenge, or action step together. Give them
something tangible to do that helps them personalize the
topic you're discussing.

Or maybe you decide that, this week, the best thing you
can do to love, influence, and care for your few is to throw
away all of your small group questions and activities and
play a game instead.

When a certain question or activity just isn't working
for my kids, I (Afton) think back to an activity they really
loved before and make it work with this lesson. One of my
group's favorites is a game we have dubbed "The Hand
Game." It's a silly name, but don't judge us, we made it
up when they were in kindergarten. The Hand Game works
great to help with memorizing Bible verses. Everyone *sits*
(HURRAY!) in a circle and puts their hands out on the floor.
You play "eeny, meeny, miny, moe" but instead you go
around saying the Bible verse, word-by-word, hand-by-
hand. The person whose hand gets the last word of the
memory verse puts that hand behind their back and we

keep going! By the end of group
all the kids can recite the memory verse and
all the kids are SITTING (and engaged) WHEN PARENTS
COME TO PICK THEM UP.

This is a win-win-win activity for my few. So think of what
your activity might be that's a win no matter what (or take
mine!) and try it out when a certain activity fails with your
few. Because sooner or later, an activity *will* fail, and it's
your job to improvise.

While activities might look different for every small group,
remember you have the freedom to improvise. Because
here's the good news—the point of your small group
conversation isn't to make it through every discussion
question. The point is to help you engage in a conversation
about authentic faith so they can better live out authentic
faith. So if you want to better engage your few by scripting
less and improvising more, try an activity!

SMALL GROUP SURVIVAL KIT: PENS & PAPER

This emergency kit item might be the more
important of all. When your conversation just
isn't working well, hand out paper and pens
to everyone! You can choose to use these
however you think works best, but you might
want to try asking them to write down their
responses on paper and giving them back to
you. Another option is that they could write
down numbers 1-5, and circle the answer they
choose. Or maybe they just need something
to do with their hands while they talk, and
doodling is the perfect solution.

3. FOLLOW RABBIT TRAILS

There will be weeks when everything seems to be going well. Your few are engaging in the conversation. The questions seem to be working. The conversation is moving.

And there will also be weeks when the conversation will take a turn you didn't expect. Maybe it's prompted by something someone said, or by what the group nearby just shouted, or by absolutely nothing at all. No matter where it comes from, it's true—more often than you'd probably like, your small group conversation will be derailed by a rabbit trail.

Most of the time, their rabbit trails will be about friends, or toys, or the video game they played that weekend. It's okay to shut them down so you can keep your conversation moving.

But *sometimes* . . . sometimes you'll come across a rabbit trail that's actually worth following.

Maybe Erin will ask a question.
Or Tricia will share something that's been happening at school.
Or Emma will tell you her mom is sick.

Not every rabbit trail is worth following, but if the rabbit trail you're dealing with . . .
is timely
is important
sparks their interest
. . . then pursue it.

Because if you want to better engage your few by scripting less and improvising more, sometimes, you'll need to follow a rabbit trail.

4. GO WITH YOUR GUT

Okay, maybe this idea of improvising makes you nervous. Maybe you like – no, *love* – having a plan. Maybe you're nervous about moving away from the plan your children's pastor gives you. Maybe you're worried you don't have permission.

If that's you, here's something to keep in mind.

No one knows your few
like you know your few.
Not even your children's pastor.

Week after week, you are the person who . . .
connects with them,
knows them,
and engages with them.
You know their lives, their worlds, their demeanors, and their backgrounds.

And since you know your few so well, it's up to you to customize your small group conversations so they work for your small group. We can give you some ideas, and your children's pastor can give you some helpful questions. But the truth is, it's up to you. If you're going to script less, and learn to improvise more, you're going to have to trust your gut, experiment, and sometimes even fail.

No one can tell you exactly how to lead your small group. Only you can do that.

So trust yourself. Because if you want to better engage your few by scripting less and improvising more, you won't have access to an instruction book. You'll need to go with your gut.

After you've prepared, connected, and gotten to know your few, if you want your small group conversations to matter more, you're going to have to engage them in a conversation. But not just any conversation—a conversation about authentic faith. That's why it's so important you learn to speak less and listen more, control less and lead more, script less and improvise more.

Because before a kid can engage in a life of authentic faith, they may need to engage in a conversation about authentic faith.

QUIZ:

HOW WELL DO YOU IMPROVISE WITH YOUR FEW?

This is a good old fashioned "bob and weave." ~~Sometimes~~ All the time you need to be flexible in your role as a small group leader. Here's a few questions to see just how flexible you can be!

On a scale of one to breaking-out-in-a-cold-sweat, how uncomfortable are you with going off-script in a small group conversation?

What are some small group questions that have totally bombed?

QUIZ

What's one way you've learned to improvise when your small group script isn't working?

Have you ever completely thrown away your script? What happened?

What's the best rabbit trail you've ever followed?

5

chapter
five
move

Move

Congratulations! You did it! You successfully engaged your small group of kids in a conversation about authentic faith!

Well, not really. You're reading a book right now. You're not leading a small group.

But let's *pretend* you've been leading a successful conversation with your small group.

And now let's imagine you're ready to wrap up that conversation.

Sure, you could wrap things up by yelling, "Okay, we're done, bye!" and sprinting for the door.

But we know you. We know you care about making your small group conversations matter more. In fact, we're pretty sure you care so much about making your small group conversations matter that you wouldn't just throw it all away in the last few moments of your time together. You're going to be strategic. You're going to finish strong.

Because it's great to engage your few in a conversation about authentic faith, but leading small group conversations isn't the only reason you signed up to be a small group leader, is it? You signed up to be a small group leader because you wanted . . .
to make a big difference.
to change the world.
to invest in a few kids so you could help them develop a lifelong, authentic kind of faith.

That's why we know you won't wrap up your small group conversation by wildly sprinting for the door.

Once you've engaged your few in a *conversation* about authentic faith, your final step is to **move your few to engage in a *life* of authentic faith.** In other words, after you've engaged them *inside* your circle, it's your job to move them to engage *outside* your circle.

So before you move for the door, here are three ways to keep your few moving toward authentic faith—even after your conversation has ended.

If you want to move your few, GIVE a next step.

When we talked about leading—not controlling—your small group conversations, we talked about the importance of keeping the end in mind. We said your ultimate . . .
destination
target
finish-line
goal
. . . isn't necessarily to help your few *remember* what they've heard. As their small group leader, your goal is to help them *apply* it.

So keep that goal in mind as you wrap up your small group conversation each week. Before you move your few out of your circle and back into the world, give them a next step. When you help them identify one simple step they can take during the week, you'll help your few learn to not only *talk* about their faith, but to *live* it out, too. So wrap up your conversation each week by asking, "What's *one* thing you're going to do this week to live this out?"

Because when you give a next step, you move them to action.

If you want to move your few, PRAY together.

You may not always have time in small group to hear from every kid about every prayer request they've ever had, but you do have time to close in prayer. Some weeks, everyone might have the opportunity to pray. Other weeks, you may only have time for one. But whether you have ten minutes or ten seconds for prayer, don't forget to pray together.

Get in the habit of asking your few for prayer requests.
Then write down their prayer requests.
And follow up on their prayer requests.

When you pray for, and with, your few, you're modeling what it looks like to talk to God, to know God, and to trust God—and that might be the only time that week a kid sees someone pray. Imagine the impact you could have on a kid's faith if your weekly small group conversations helped them have better conversations, not just their small group, but with the God who made them.

Because when you pray together, you move your few toward God.

The very first Sunday with my small group, I Afton, made sure to make prayer a priority. I told them we would do this each week, and that I'd ask them each week if there's anything specific I can pray for them about. After a few submissions like, "That it will snow!" (in August . . . in the South) and "That we would have good dreams," I told them all to get close, and huddle up for our prayer.

Now this was my fault, I'll admit. Because I did use the term "huddle up." But before I realized exactly what was happening, all twelve of my kindergarteners were dog-piled together on the floor in front of me. They were ready to pray. So . . . I went with it! Because here's something important to remember: they are *kids*, and I want to encourage them that they can pray in whatever way works for them. The odds of me getting all of them to fold their hands and sit criss-cross applesauce for fifteen whole seconds are slim. But getting them to dog pile for thirty seconds to pray . . . well, I think that's a win.

If you want to move your few, SAY something meaningful.

If you've led well, you've probably spent most of your small group conversation asking questions, listening, and asking more questions. But as your small group conversation comes to a close, and your few are preparing to leave the safe place of your small group for another week, you have the opportunity to say something meaningful—something that has the potential to stay with them all week long.

Like . . .
"I love you guys."
"I'm praying for you."
"I'm here for you."
"I believe in you."

When you say something meaningful to your few, you help them feel significant. Who knows the impact those words might have on even one kid in your group. After all, a few words can make a big difference in the direction of someone's life.

So before you move your few out of your circle, choose your words wisely. Say something meaningful. When you do, you'll move them toward significance.

As you wrap up your small group conversation, finish strong. When you give a next step, pray together, and say something meaningful, you help your few **move**—not just out of your circle, but into a life of more authentic faith.

conclusion

Conclusion

So if you want to have better conversations with the kids in your small group . . .

PREPARE for the conversation you'll have in your circle.
CONNECT with your few and help them connect with each other.
KNOW your few and help them know each other.
ENGAGE your few by speaking less, listening more, controlling less, leading more, scripting less, and improvising more.
MOVE your few toward a life of authentic faith outside your circle.

That's not easy. Leading conversations with kids can still be difficult, no matter how well you prepare, connect, know, engage, or move your few. Sometimes . . .
they'll still be distracted.
you'll still ask a question that bombs.
they'll still sit in silence.
you'll still lose control.
they'll still ask questions you can't answer.
you'll still wonder who put you in charge.

We probably haven't answered all of your questions.
We probably haven't solved all of your problems.
But we hope we've shared at least a few stories, ideas, and strategies that will help you make your next small group conversation a little more effective.

So this week . . .
Prepare
Connect
Know
Engage
Move.

And remember . . .

Every conversation with your small group matters. But you can make this week's conversation matter even more.

author bios

Author bios

AFTON PHILLIPS

Afton Phillips is the Lead Small Director at Orange—which basically means she has been thinking about small groups, small group leaders, and small group strategies since every single day since 2012. Before that, she spent three years working in children's ministry at Browns Bridge Church and graduated from Johnson University with a degree in Children's Ministry. But most importantly, Afton leads a small group of 2nd graders every Sunday. If you want to be Afton's best friend, all you need to do is buy her a black coffee and let her wear a tiara all day. She strongly believes tulle skirts should be worn every single day and her favorite place is any giant used book store.

ADAM DUCKWORTH

Adam Duckworth is the Lead Communicator at Downtown Harbor Church in Fort Lauderdale, FL. He transitioned to this role after spending nearly 15 years in family ministry. He is also one of the authors of "Not Normal" and " Leading Not Normal Volunteers" alongside Sue Miller. Additionally, he is the Owner of Travelmation, LLC, which is an Authorized Disney Vacation Planner which exists to help families make magical memories. His favorite attraction is the Country Bear Jamboree.

LEARN MORE
ABOUT LEAD SMALL
+
DOWNLOAD OUR
UBERCOOL AMAZING
FREE APP
@ LEADSMALL.ORG